THOU ART BEAUTIFUL

Becoming a
Kingdom Confident
Woman
in 30 Days

L. FONVILLE

Global Press Publishing

Thou Art Beautiful
© *2021 by LaToya Fonville*

This book is also available as an e-book.
Visit www.ThouArtBeautiful.org

Request for information should be addressed to:
World Press Publishing,
701 Seneca St., Suite, 777, Buffalo, NY 14210.
ISBN: 978-1-7372740-0-1
E-Book ISBN: 978-1-7372740-1-8

Library of Congress Control Number: 2021939562
This book is printed on acid-free paper.

Cover Design: LCP Visual Artistry & Graphics
Interior Design: Daniel Ojedokun
Editor: CTL WriteRight, LLC.

Printed in the United States of America

FOREWARD

When LaToya approached me about writing the Foreword for this book, I was more than happy to oblige. It's not hard to write the "before" word for a book that will not only provide inspirational reading, but literally transform the way you see yourself and show up in the world.

I am a trained psychologist. For over a decade I worked with survivors of childhood sexual abuse, mostly women. The devastation of enduring years of shame for the evil that was done against them was apparent in the way they talked, moved, and engaged the world. I can recall one woman using the term, "I'm damaged goods." When encouraged to expand on that thought she shared this analogy. Of all the perfect, undented canned goods in the grocery store she considered herself the damaged one. The one that was unusual; the one that was passed over and eventually discarded. How sad to think that one could live believing she was damaged goods; one day to be discarded and ineligible for redemption.

Another woman who came to me in her sixties, considered herself "less than." Secretly blaming herself for the childhood abuse she encountered and constantly trying to work to receive God's love. One day, she reported with joy, "Do you know that I am the apple of God's eye?" Of course, I said yes. Then she happily shared the scripture in Zechariah 2:8 that reads, "For thus says the Lord of hosts: "He sent Me after glory, to the nations which plunder you; for he who touches you touches the apple of His eye." She sat there gleaming that day, finally knowing the truth that made her free: she was loved and the apple of God's eye.

God wants you free too. That's why He has sent LaToya for such a time as this. In the pages of this book, find your freedom! As you read chapters like I am ROYALTY, I am PERFECTION, and I am HEALED, give God permission to wash you clean from every damaging lie that has threatened to destroy your existence. This is your time to flourish, shine, and be ALL that He ordained before the foundations of the earth.

You may not know it now, but this is a divine setup. God is moving on your behalf and is rejoicing in heaven knowing that within the next 30 days you will know how beautiful you are and finally become the Kingdom Confident woman you were created to be.

Know that life is a journey and being free from lies is a process, however if you stick with this book, I believe by the end you will know that, Thou Art Beautiful.

Dr. Celeste Owens
Founder, Surrender 365, INC.

ACKNOWLEDGMENTS

Thank you:

Lord; for entrusting me with this great assignment. Millions of Women will be transformed, delivered and set free.

Babe; my amazing husband, Stewart, for the laughter and balance you bring to my life. Thank you for always encouraging me and stretching me to strive for greater and better.

Maximilian, Marc Anthony and Matthias; my amazing boys. Your presence in my life has caused me to be to grow in ways I've never imagined. I thank God for my World Changers.

Rudy & Marie Dorsett; Daddy, you have always been a pillar of strengths and wisdom, you taught me my value and worth. Thank you for always being there. Mommy, you taught me how to pray, you pushed me beyond my comfort zone and you demanded only the best from me. I am here today because of you and

I thank you mommy.

Sonya; my mother in love, thank you for daily covering us in prayer, thank you for the fun you bring to our lives. More importantly the great example you are as a faithful intercessor.

Supt. Donald Chisholm; Sr. aka "Uncle D;" You were my pastor, my mentor and an example of what it means to trust in the Lord. You thought me to what Radical Faith is and how to truly lean on the Lord. I love you and miss you dearly.

Bishop Michael Badger; Bishop you pulled me out of religion taught me relationship. Under your leadership my life was radically transformed and God became real to me. The foundation for my faith today was fortified under your life changing preaching and I am eternally grateful for you.

Evangelist Lynne Parker; My dearest friend, mentor and anointed Graphic Designer. Thank you for your prayers, words of encouragement and patience as we labored to bring this vision to life.

Table of Contents

INTRODUCTION

I am LaToya Fonville, founder of The Thou Art Beautiful Movement. I would like to congratulate you on investing in yourself and your future. The Thou Art Beautiful 30-Day Transformation Series is a Holy Ghost-inspired devotional that will build your self-image, reestablish your God-given identity, and realign your vision in order for you to see yourself the way that God sees you. It's time for you to know who God says you are.

1 Peter 2:9 lets us know that, "You are a chosen generation, a royal priesthood, a holy nation." Do you know that you are somebody to God? Throughout the Bible, there are scriptures that show God affirming your identity and reminding you of who you are to Him. The scriptures reveal why He created you, as well as the great plans He has for you. You were destined by God to be here, and your life has meaning and great significance.

I don't know about you, but since my childhood, the enemy showed up in my life and tried to destroy the very essence of who God said I am and what He said I was created to do.

Repeatedly, the lie that: I was a mistake. I was not good enough. I was ugly. Constantly bombarded my thoughts. I felt as if my existence didn't matter. And I can go on and on. I am sure that you could fill in the blanks with all the lies that the devil has repeatedly spoken over your life.

You see, you must understand that God's Word warns us in John 10:10 that, "The thief comes not but to steal, kill and destroy (KJV)." Yes, I must repeat: the devil comes to steal, kill and destroy your identity, your destiny—even the very purpose that God has ordained for your life. If you don't know who God says that you are, then you become a hopeless wanderer on the Ferris wheel of life—going round and round in the same cycle of hopelessness, despair, defeat, and lies.

The Thou Art Beautiful 30-Day Transformation Series will begin to dispel the lies and reaffirm the truth according to the Word of God. Each day, I will walk you through a declaration from my "Thou Art Beautiful" Affirmation Deck. These are the very words that the Lord spoke into my character to resurrect me from the bed of lies that kept me bound, and catapulted me into my destiny.

Today I speak on national and international platforms. I coach aspiring entrepreneurs, corporate professionals, and many others. I give God the glory for that. This shy, introverted girl with low self-esteem, who once stuttered, has faced her fears. I have overcome the lies through declaring and activating the Word of God, and have now been transformed into His image—the image of the Father. So, get ready to embark on a journey of transformation. It's time for you to see yourself through God's eyes and become all that God has created you to be.

If you're interested in purchasing the "Thou Art Beautiful" Affirmation Deck or want to learn more information about any of my coaching programs, visit me at ThouArtBeautiful. org, so we can develop a customized strategy to unleash the God-ordained destiny that is waiting to be released within you.

If you are ready to be free—if you are ready to walk in confidence and see yourself through God's eyes—let's begin this journey. I'm so excited! However, I must warn you: the devil will not be happy about this. Therefore, you must begin to intercede on behalf of yourself to stop the plan of the enemy. You must make a resolve that you will persevere in spite of the obstacles and stumbling blocks that will come your way. Remember: your life is on the line.

Prayer of Activation

Father God, in the mighty and matchless Name of Jesus: I come before You, Lord, to glorify You, to exalt Your name, and to magnify You. I take dominion over the atmosphere of the environments of our homes, our offices, our vehicles, and over our lives. Father, I pray that as Your daughter goes through this step-by-step, day-by-day journey of change and transformation, that she will begin to take on the characteristics of the Kingdom and will begin to walk in Kingdom confidence. Father, I welcome You into each day. I welcome You into our minds, dear Lord. Father, I thank You for Your transforming power. I thank You for Your renewing power. I thank You for Your grace and Your mercy. Father, cover Your daughter as she reads this, and let Your glory—Your yoke-destroying, destiny-activating, life-transforming glory rest upon her, to bring about change and to release Your daughter into her destiny. Father, lead and guide her as she goes through each day. Lord, come into her heart and mind so that she can pick up the broken pieces of her life and create a masterpiece. God, I know that You have created her to do something great and extraordinary. So Father, bless your daughter right now and cover her, keep her, and protect her. This I pray in Jesus' Name. Amen.

For the next 30 days, you will be going through a daily declaration from my "Thou Art Beautiful" Affirmation Deck. Remember it is essential to meditate on each declaration and allow the Holy Spirit to begin to move within you to bring about transformation. Be Blessed!

Day

1

I AM ROYALTY

"You are a chosen generation,
a royal priesthood, a holy nation."
1 Peter 2:9a

You are royalty! Repeat after me: I am royalty! I really want you to get that in your spirit. I am royalty. 1 Peter 2:9 says, "You are a chosen generation, a royal priesthood, a holy nation." I want you to understand and know that you are chosen by God. You are royalty. You are holy and unique in all your ways.

If life has told you that you are anything contrary to that truth, then it was a lie straight from the pit of hell. I need you to understand that when you walk in a room, the very essence of your character screams royalty. When you open your mouth, the intonations and the inflections of your voice speak royalty. The very nature of who God created you to be is royalty. I don't care what you've done, what has happened in your life, or what lies the enemy continues to superimpose in your mind. That is a lie. And I need you to know that you are forgiven, you are redeemed, and you are royalty.

Prayer of Activation

Father God, right now in the mighty and matchless Name of Jesus, I come before You just to say thank You. Lord I thank You for my life, I thank You for the great plans that You have for my life, and I thank You for this road map to deliverance. Father God, right now I uproot and dismantle every lie that has been spoken into my character that has told me that I am not royalty. Father, I come against every lie and every agenda sent to dethrone me from my position of authority. Father God, I decree and declare that from this day forth, that I shall rise up. I shall go forth and be all that You have created me to be. I thank You, Lord, that from this day forth that I am redeemed. I am set free. I am renewed. I am royalty. Lord, I bless Your Holy Name and I seal this prayer in Jesus' Name. Amen.

Remember to meditate on that word throughout the day: you are royalty. Remember to begin to apply it in your life, through everything that you do. If anything comes your way that is opposite of that truth, you now know that it's a lie and you no longer have to receive it as a truth in your life because: you are royalty.

Day 2

I AM GORGEOUS

Today I want to remind you and let you know that God the Father—our Daddy—said that you are gorgeous. I need you to repeat after me: I am gorgeous! Now look at yourself in the mirror, touch your heart and say: I am gorgeous. I am gorgeous. Yes, I'm talking about you. Yes, you are gorgeous.

Song of Solomon 4:7 says that, "You are altogether beautiful, my darling; there is no flaw in you (NIV)." This is what the Father says about you. I don't care if they said that you're "too dark," or "too light"; "too short," or "too tall"; your nose is "too narrow," or "too wide"; your lips are "too thin," or "too thick"; your eyes are "too small," or "too large." I don't care what was said about you. It is not true. God the Father—the creator of heaven and earth, and all that is seen and unseen—said that you are altogether beautiful, my darling. He's saying, "My love, you're beautiful, you're gorgeous; there's no flaw in you."

Remember that you were created in the image and the likeness of God the Father. You look like your Daddy. You are flawless. You're perfect. You are spectacular. You are superb. You are wonderful. You are impressive—all combined in one gorgeous package. Yes, darling, I'm talking about you. You are gorgeous—not because I said so, but because God the Father said so. I need you to meditate on that throughout the day. I need you to think about that. I need you to know and understand that: yes, my Daddy says that I am gorgeous.

If someone says something contrary to that today, say, "no, that's not true. I'm gorgeous." I want you to begin to dispel the lies that you believe about yourself. Remember, God does not make mistakes, and nothing about your make up is a mistake. Stop comparing yourself to the airbrushed icons portrayed in the media. Stop comparing yourself to others, or to your younger body, or your body before kids. You are in a league of your own and no one can measure up to all that God has placed in and throughout you. I really want you to get that into your spirit. Girl! You really are gorgeous!

Prayer of Activation

Father God, I come before Your wonderous throne and I pray that You would open my eyes so that I will begin to see myself as You see me, God. Today, I remove the veil of lies that have been seeded into my spirit from childhood. I denounce every word-curse that has ever been spoken over my character about the very beauty that You have given me. And today, God, I decree and declare that I am released, I am set free, and my vision has been adjusted so that I can begin to see myself the way You see me, as gorgeous.

Father, I thank You that I now open my eyes and see the very beauty that you have strategically and intricately put together in my mother's womb. You made no mistake when You created me. You stepped back and said, "This is good." So Father, I thank You because I am Your gorgeous creation.

Father God, I bind every lie of the enemy that may bombard my thoughts throughout this day. I denounce its effects over my life. I decree and declare that from this day forth that I am liberated, set free, and I now begin to see myself as You see me: gorgeous! Father, I bless You and praise You in Jesus' Name. Amen.

Now throughout today, I want you to continue to meditate on that declaration. I am gorgeous. Because girl, you are gorgeous. That's what Daddy says. Begin to meditate on that. Begin to lean on that. Begin to focus on that throughout the day. If any thoughts come up that are contrary to that truth, respond and say, "No, that is not of God. I am gorgeous."

Day

3

I AM AMAZING

"For we are His workmanship, created in Christ Jesus unto good works, which God prepared beforehand that we should walk in them."

Ephesians 2:10

Do you know that the Father says that you are amazing? Repeat after me. "I am amazing." Just stay right there for a second. Think about that. I am amazing. Say it again: "I am amazing." Yes, I'm amazing. I need you to know that you are amazing.

Ephesians 2:10 says, "For we are His workmanship, created in Christ Jesus unto good works, which God prepared beforehand that we should walk in them." Again, it says, "For we are His workmanship, created in Christ Jesus..." Think about a master craftsman intricately putting together a project. That craftsman takes his time and ponders over every detail of every aspect of his creation, and he won't stop until it is perfect. God, just like the craftsman, took His time when He created you. He said, "I'm going to make her amazing. I'm not going to rush this project."

When God created you, He didn't just go 1-2-3-boom, and there you were. No! When He forged the very personality that makes you uniquely you, He took his time, and then He paused and said, "Wow. That's amazing." When He gave you your quirks and habits, the very things that set you apart from others, He took his time and He said, "Yes that's amazing." I need you to know and understand that when the Father looks upon you, He sees nothing but His amazing creation. He sees His masterpiece—you—and He delights in that. I need you to understand, I need you to remember, and I need you to get that in your spirit: you are amazing.

Prayer of Activation

Father God, in the Name of Jesus, I come before You today—coming into agreement with Your truth that I am the masterpiece that You have created me to be. Not average, not subpar, but absolutely amazing. Father God, thank You that I am Your workmanship, created in Christ Jesus, to do great and marvelous works. I thank You, Father, that heaven cries out and declares that I am amazing. I decree that from this day forth, I am redeemed, I am released, and I am set free to go forth and be the amazing, unique creation that You have created me to be. I thank You, Father, that I am the manifestation of Your workmanship—Your masterpiece created to do great and marvelous works. I thank You Father God, that from this day forth that I will see myself as amazing. Amen.

Remember, the Lord says, "you are amazing." Throughout this day, continue to declare that into the atmosphere. Continue to remind yourself that God says, "you are amazing."

Day
4

I AM DELIGHTFUL

"God saw all that He had made,
and indeed it was very good."
Genesis 1:31a

You are delightful. Repeat after me: "I am delightful." I need you to know that you are delightful. You bring joy to everyone around you, and your presence—yes, your presence—brightens up the room. Genesis 1:31 says, "God saw all that He had made, and indeed it was very good." See, when God created you, when He created humanity,

He stepped back and pondered on it for a second and said, "This is good." Yes, when God created you, He thought about it, and He was very pleased with the outcome of His work. So when God sees you, He sees His creation. He sees a woman. He sees His beloved daughter in whom He delights. When God looks at you, it brings Him joy.

Another word for delightful according to thesaurus.com is pleasing, pleasant, agreeable, lovely, adorable, appealing, attractive and good-looking1. Yes, that's exactly how God describes you. That's how God sees you. This is how you must begin to see yourself—because the very essence of who you are is pleasing, pleasant, agreeable, kind, endearing, lovely, and that's just the beginning. This is who you are. Just know that you are delightful. As I said before, I will say it again: your very presence brings joy to everyone around you, and you brighten up the room. Today I need you to meditate on that. I need you to live it out. I need you to activate that and become the pleasing, agreeable and loving person that God has created you to be: delightful.

Prayer of Activation

Father, in the name of Jesus, I speak to every root of bitterness that has affected the very essence of who You created me to be. Father, I know that deep down I am sweet, charming, loving, agreeable, and yes, delightful. Lord, if any situation or circumstance has tarnished my character, if any situation has made me untrusting, or if anything has made me contrary to being the delightful woman of God You created me to be, I uproot the effect of that situation and that trauma right now in the name of Jesus. I decree and declare that Your love will encompass me, Your peace will surround me, and Your glory will rest upon me so that I may be the light in the midst of darkness. Father, I come in agreement with Your Word and I declare that I am no longer my past, but I am liberated by the blood of Jesus. I am set free to be the delightsome beauty that You have created me to be. Father, I thank You for Your healing power. Today, I welcome Your transforming power into my heart and my mind. Lord, let Your anointing and authority be released into my life so that I can go forth and be the joy that You have made me to be. Thank You, Lord. I seal this prayer in Jesus' Name. Amen.

I want to thank you for committing to your own deliverance. I need you to continue to meditate on the fact that you are delightful. If you see anything in you that is opposite of that, I need you to go back and release the people who have hurt you. Release them so that you can be set free and become the joy that God has designed and created you to be—because your presence really does light up the world. Remember: you are delightful.

Day 5

I AM BEAUTIFUL

*"God created man in His own image.
In the image of God He created him;
male and female He created them."*
Genesis 1:27

Today I want you to receive this truth: you are beautiful! I will repeat it again: you are beautiful. Yes, you are beautiful. Now, repeat after me and internalize this: "I am beautiful." Genesis 1:27 says, "God created man in His own image. In the image of God He created him; male and female He created them." Let's read that again. "God created man in His own image. In the image of God He created him; male and female He created them." You look just like your Father. You're beautiful. You look like the Creator of all that is seen and unseen, the Alpha, the Omega, the King of all kings, the Lord of all lords. You look like your Daddy. You need to know that you really are beautiful.

Today, I want you to surrender the hurt of the trauma that you have experienced in your life. Jesus became a curse that you might be a blessing (Galatians 3:13). You have been redeemed by the shed blood of Jesus. Therefore, you no longer have to relive the torment of that moment. Right now, I want you to take a moment and give it to God. Release the hurt, release the pain, and give it to God. The trauma of the situation you encountered opened the door for the enemy to come in and intercept your identity. You've been a victim of identity theft and the devil has deceived you to into believing that you are not the daughter of the Most High God. We know that is a lie. God says in Genesis 1:27 that you are created in His image. His Word says, "male and female, He created him." God created you, and you are exactly who your Heavenly Father says you are: beautiful.

Right now, I denounce all the trauma that you have experienced in your life, and I denounce all side effects associated with that moment that has immobilized you and tainted your self-image. I pray for healing over your mind and body and I pray for total deliverance from that event, right now in Jesus' Name. Amen.

I need you to know and understand that you are created in the image and likeness of God, and you are beautiful. God does not make mess, and He definitely does not make mistakes. I pray that you are liberated to begin seeing yourself as the beautiful creation that God has intricately and uniquely woven in your mother's womb. Remember, you look like your Father, the Creator of heaven and earth, and you are blessed by Him. Therefore, you are beautiful—because God took His time when He created you.

Prayer of Activation

Father God, in the Name of Jesus, I come before You to ask for strength as I walk through this process of becoming whole. Father, we know that You said in Your word that all things (that means even the terrible things) will work together for good (Romans 8:28). I thank You, God, because out of the broken pieces of my life, You are creating a magnificent masterpiece. Father, you also said that the sufferings of this present time are not worthy to be compared to the glory that is to be revealed (Romans 8:18). Thank You Lord, because for every tear that I have shed, you are replacing it with joy. I decree and declare that from this moment forward, I will see myself through a new lens. I thank You Lord, because when I look in the mirror, I see myself as your beautiful creation: hand-crafted, hand-picked, and hand-selected by the

King of all kings and the Lord of all lords. Thank You Lord, because I now see myself for who I really am: Your fearfully and wonderfully made masterpiece. I thank you for the deliverance taking place in me right now. I thank You Lord, because even my vision has been transformed. Today is a new day for me, and I walk in my deliverance as God's beautiful creation: renewed, refreshed, and revived. I seal this prayer in Jesus' Name. Amen.

Today I need you to walk through a process of forgiveness. In order for you to begin to truly see yourself as beautiful, just the way God sees you, you have to begin to release the hurt, the bitterness, and the pain of what happened. No one can ever understand the gravity of your experience. But I know one Man who does: His name is Jesus Christ. He died on the Cross. He was beaten, mocked, and put to shame. He took on your pain so you could be free. Only God understands your pain, and He has the power to make you whole. Even on the Cross, Jesus forgave His persecutors. So today, I urge you to begin to release those people who victimized you. Release those people who hurt you. Release those who turned their backs on you—so that you can see yourself the way God sees you. Then, when you open your eyes and look in the mirror, you will begin to behold the beauty of God's very creation. Then, you will know and understand that you really are beautiful.

I AM INTELLIGENT

"Now the all earth sought the presence of Solomon to hear his wisdom, which God had put in his heart."
1 Kings 10:24

Today I want you to know that you are intelligent. Repeat after me: "I am intelligent. I am smart. I am wise. I can do anything because I am grounded and rooted in Christ. Yes, I am intelligent." 1 Kings 10:24 says, "Now all the earth sought the presence of Solomon to hear his wisdom, which God had put in his heart." When you look at the scriptural meaning of heart, it means mind. Wisdom, knowledge and understanding are given to us by God. As believers, we have a competitive advantage over the world, and we have divine insight. We can go straight to God, the Father, and ask Him to give us intelligence, creativity, solutions, or strategy.

I need you to understand that you are intelligent, even if the school system put you in special education classes, or if you struggled with dyslexia, or any type of mind-related challenges or that society may deem as disorders. I need you to understand that when God created you, He made no mistake. So don't put yourself in a box and say, "Well, I am this. I am that." No, I need you to know that you are intelligent, because the Father says that you are intelligent. God asked Solomon, "What do you want?" And he said, "Give me wisdom." When God gave him wisdom, He gave him everything. People from the North, South, East, and West—kings and queens—sought after King Solomon: to get his wisdom and hear what he had to say. And just like Solomon, you have the ability to go directly to the throne of God. You have the ability to go boldly before the throne, to the Father, and ask what you will. So if you need intelligence—if you've been lied to and were told that you're not smart enough or you're not good enough—then I need you to go before God and begin to intercede and ask for wisdom, ask for knowledge, and ask for intelligence. He will give it to you freely.

Prayer of Activation

Father God, in the Name of Jesus, I come against every lie that has ever been spoken over me, telling me that I am not smart enough, I am not good enough, or that I am incapable of achieving greater. I come against it, and I dismantle that lie right now in the Name of Jesus. Lord, I declare that I am set free from every lie spoken over this great mind that You have given me. Lord, release wisdom from the Kingdom of heaven upon me. Lord, release creativity, release solutions to major problems that will transform societies. Lord release cures that will destroy cancer and incurable diseases. Lord, thank You that I can boldly come before your throne and ask for wisdom and understanding, so that I can operate in ultimate intelligence, as You have destined for me. Father, I seal this prayer in the Name of Jesus, and I decree and declare that any lie that I was not smart enough or not good enough, has been dismantled and destroyed, from this day forth. I shall go forth and be the intelligent woman that you have created me to be. This I pray in Jesus' Name, Amen.

Throughout this day, I need you to begin to speak over yourself and remind yourself of who God says you are. Even if you tell yourself, "I'm not good enough, I can't do that." Begin to do the opposite of that—and remember that you are intelligent.

I AM SOPHISTICATED

*"For the Lord Gives wisdom; from
His mouth come knowledge and understanding."*
Proverbs 2:6

Today I want you to know that you are sophisticated. Yes, you are sophisticated. Repeat after me: "I am sophisticated." A synonym for sophisticated, according to Dictionary. com is knowledgeable1. You are knowledgeable, you are intelligent, and you are sophisticated. Proverbs 2:6 says, "For the Lord Gives wisdom; from His mouth come knowledge and understanding." You are sophisticated, classy, honorable, and one in a million. There's no one on this earth as authentic and unique as you. The more sophisticated you is hidden in your deeper relationship with the Father. Yes, that's the secret.

Do you want to be known as that sophisticated, classy, honorable woman, who makes a greater impact on society? Then it's time for you to step up your prayer life. It is time for you to step up your devotional time. It is time for you to step up your time in the presence of the Father—because it is in His presence that He will give you wisdom straight from heaven. It is in the presence of the Lord, where He will give you knowledge and reveal deep and hidden things (Daniel 2:22). The mysteries that the Lord will reveal to you, when you get into that secret place, will confound the mind of man. People will be in awe and wonder, saying, "Wow, how does she know this?"

Imagine being in such a place with God that He has refined you to the point where people are coming to you for advice, people are coming to you for wisdom. That type of power only comes from your time with the Lord, that comes from being intimate with the Father. You want to be sophisticated? Then it's time for you to spend more time in the presence of the Lord. Today, I want you to know that God says that you are sophisticated, you are classy, you are honorable, and you are one in a million. There's no one else that will ever touch this earth who will be as awesome and amazing as you. You put a spin on sophistication that no one else can. So don't allow life or the lies of the enemy to taint you or change who you are. That smile that God gave you? Continue to let it shine. That laugh that shifts the atmosphere—that contagious one? Yes, God gave you that laugh. God made you who you are, so don't change it. You are sophisticated, you are knowledgeable, and you have wisdom from the Father Himself.

Prayer of Activation

Father God, I come before You today thanking You because I am validated by You. I thank You for showing me who I am in You. You created me in the womb, Lord. You gave me understanding and knowledge. You gave me direction and guidance. Father, You orchestrated my life and You have brought me a mighty long way. Lord, I thank You that I am no longer a victim of the lies that were spoken over my life—nor am I bound by the negative thoughts that once controlled my mind. Instead, I am liberated through Christ Jesus. Amen.2

Romans 12:2 says, "Be not conformed to this world: but be ye transformed by the renewing of your mind (KJV)." Thank you, Lord, that my mind is renewed. I operate in wisdom, knowledge, and understanding. Everywhere I go, doors open for me that no man can shut. Father, I glorify Your Holy Name, and I thank You and praise You, because You made me special, unique, and sophisticated in Jesus' Name. Amen.

I want you to remember that it is only when you get in the presence of God that He will reveal answers, solutions, ideas, and knowledge that will give you an advantage in everything that you do. So, keep God first in your life, and the knowledge of God will radically transform your life. I want you to get this into your spirit: you are sophisticated, you are knowledgeable, and you have wisdom given to you from God Himself.

I AM PERFECTION

*"Therefore you shall be perfect, just as
your Father in heaven is perfect."*
Matthew 5:48

According to Dictionary.com, perfect means conforming absolutely to the description or definition of an ideal type1. You are made in the image and likeness of God the Father Himself. You are the essence of God's perfection. Repeat after me: "I am perfect. I am perfection." Put your hand on your chest and say it to yourself: "I am perfect." Matthew

5:48 says, "Therefore you shall be perfect, just as your Father in heaven is perfect." You have to be just like your Father. In Christ, you are perfect—nothing missing, nothing broken. You are perfect.

This is what the Father says. You are made in His image and likeness. Therefore, you are like Him. The characteristics and the traits that you possess mimic that of your heavenly Father. And remember that Matthew 5:48 says, "Therefore you shall be perfect, just as your Father in heaven is perfect." I need you to understand that you are perfect. You are the essence of God's divine perfection in Christ. I want to pause for a moment and address the woman reading this book who has not taken that step and given her life to Christ. If you have not accepted Jesus Christ as your Lord and Savior, then you're missing out on all of these blessings.

In Christ, you are perfect—nothing missing, nothing broken. In Christ, you have direct access to the Father. In Christ, you can now go boldly before the throne of grace. In Christ, all things have passed away and all things have become new. In Christ, you have a fresh start and a new beginning. You can start over.

Now, we've all made mistakes. The Bible says that we all fall short of His glory. We all make mistakes, and yet, God still calls us perfect. He says that we are to be perfect, just as our Heavenly Father is perfect. The only way that we can be made perfect is if we take that first step and accept Jesus Christ as our Lord and Savior. Believe that He died on the cross for your sins. And confess that He is Lord. Make a commitment today to allow Christ to come into your heart. Make that commitment today to transform your lifestyle and allow God in His perfection, in His authority, in His awesomeness, to make you perfect, unique, set apart, and great in Him.

Prayer of Activation

Heavenly Father, I come to You today asking that You change my ways, my thoughts and my heart so that I can be more like You. I pray, Lord, that You are transforming, renewing and reshaping my mind so that I may be confirmed to Your perfect will for my life. Today, I declare that in Christ I am perfect—nothing missing, nothing broken. I decree and declare that I am capable of achieving what seems impossible, and that everything that I touch prospers. I declare that every place where the soles of my feet tread is blessed. Today, I stand on Your truth that in Christ, I am perfect. Father, I thank You that when You look upon me, You don't see my sins. You don't see my shortcomings. You see Christ. And in Christ, Father God, You see a perfect being. Me. So I thank You for sending Your son Jesus Christ. In Him, I have been made perfect. Thank You Lord, because I am saved, my life is transformed, and I am a new creation in Christ. From this day forward, I am no longer on the track of failure, demise or defeat. Lord, You are catapulting me into my destiny to be great, to be awesome, and to do miraculous works for the glory of Your Name. Father, I bless You, I thank You and I praise You, in Jesus' Name. Amen.

Throughout this day, I want you to continue to meditate on that word—because in Christ, you really are perfect. You have the ability to be perfect, just like your Heavenly Father is perfect, as it is written in Matthew 5:48.

I AM LOVELY

"Finally, brethren, whatever things are true, whatever things are noble, whatever things are just, whatever things are pure, whatever things are lovely, whatever things are of good report, if there is any virtue and if there is anything praiseworthy— meditate on these things."

Philippians 4:8

Today, I want you to ponder on the unique traits that you possess that make you special. These qualities are the ones that only you can bring to this world, and it sets you apart from everyone else around you. Today, I want you to stop and realize that you are lovely. Yes, you are lovely. Say to yourself, "I am lovely. I am absolutely lovely." Philippians, 4:8 says, "Finally, brethren, whatever things are true, whatever things are noble, whatever things are just, whatever things are pure, whatever things are lovely, whatever things are of good report, if there is any virtue and if there is anything praiseworthy—meditate on these things." I need you to know that you are loved by God, and by everyone who has the honor of meeting you. Your life is worth living and you are worth loving. I repeat: you are loved by God, and every single person who has the honor of meeting you. Your life is worth living, and you are worth loving. That's the truth and that is a fact.

If the people in your life at this current moment do not uphold those standards, then you need to change your associations. There is a saying that you are the average of the five people you hang around the most. So if the people in your circle are not edifying you—if they don't honor the good characteristics and the qualities within you, or if they don't see you as lovely—then you need to think about who you're calling your friends. God calls you lovely. God tells you to think on things that are uplifting, that are true, that bring joy into your life—to think on those things. Anything that is opposite of that is not of God; it doesn't breathe life and it doesn't breathe hope. I need you to know who God said that you are, and I need you to begin to stand on that. Today, I just want to remind you that you are lovely.

Prayer of Activation

Father, I come before You, taking this moment to thank You for loving me so much that You gave Your only Son to die on the Cross so that I might have an abundant life. Thank you, Lord, for first loving me so that I would know how to love. Father, I thank You that You call me lovely. Therefore, I am lovely. Father, I just bless You and I praise you and I glorify Your Name. In Jesus' Name I pray. Amen.

Remember: you are lovely. Begin to think on that and exude that in everything that you do.

Day
10

I AM WONDERFUL

"I will praise You, for I am fearfully and wonderfully
made: marvelous are Your works, and that
my soul knows very well."
Psalm 139:14

Your Heavenly Father, the Creator of heaven and earth, the Creator of all that is seen and unseen says that, "You are wonderful." Psalms 139:14 declares, "I will praise You, for I am fearfully and wonderfully made: marvelous are Your works, and that my soul knows very well." God calls you

His marvelous work. God said that you are fearfully and wonderfully made. Wonderful in Hebrew is Pala, which means marvelous, separate, set apart.

I don't know if you were like me, but I was the "different" kid in my family. I was the one that was set apart, in a sense. I didn't fit in with my brothers and sister. I was different. I was wonderful. Just like me, God has created you differently. He has set you apart, He has made you unique for a reason. You are Pala; you are wonderful. According to the Word of God, you are marvelous; your ways are marvelous, and your actions are marvelous. The unique things about you separate you and set you apart. God created you that way because there is a set assignment that He has for you to accomplish on the earth. So, don't try to be like everyone else. Don't try to do things like everyone else. You are different for a reason. So begin to love that part of you. Begin to appreciate it and begin to praise God—because He didn't make you like everyone else. He made you wonderful. He made you separate. He made you set apart.

I want you to think about Joseph. He was different from his brothers. He was set apart. He was called to do something great in the earth. And his own family couldn't even understand him. They didn't even appreciate the gift that he was. To make a long story short, he was sold into slavery and he was imprisoned. But at the end, it all worked out for good. He ended up being second-in-command in

Egypt. God has a plan for your life. And He made you different for a reason. He separated you from everyone else because He has a unique assignment for your life. So don't begin to think that it is a problem. Don't allow the enemy to make you believe that your unique characteristics are bad things. That is a lie, I tell you. I need you to know today that you are wonderful. The Word says in Psalm 139 that you are wonderful. You are Pala. You are marvelous, you are separate. You are set apart.

Prayer of Activation

Father, I thank You because You said in Your word that I am fearfully and wonderfully made. I thank You Father, because the plan that you have for my life is good. I thank You Lord, because no weapon formed against me shall prosper (Isaiah 54:17). With Joseph, who was rejected from his family, You created something great out of his life. Just like Joseph, Lord, You are taking my pain, my rejection, and my abandonment, and you are making something great and something wonderful out of my life. I thank You Lord, because You were there when I was isolated, and you gave me the strength to press forward. Father, Your word says in Jeremiah 29:11 that You have a great plan for my life and it is good; that you have an assignment for my life; and the way you created me was not by accident, but it was wonderful. So Lord, I pray for peace in my mind. I pray for strength in my body to continue to run this race. Lord, cover and keep me; lead me and guide me, God. And just like Joseph, in due season, elevate me—display and glorify Yourself through me. I seal this prayer in Jesus' Name. Amen.

Throughout the day, I want you to begin to remember that the Lord said that you are marvelous and set apart. You are wonderful and I need you to know that. Let that be a part of your spirit. Begin to speak that throughout your day: I am wonderful.

Day
11

I AM CAPABLE

*"I can do all things through
Christ who strengthens me."*
Philippians 4:13

"…With God, all things are possible."
Matthew 19:26b

Repeat after me: "I am capable. I can do the impossible. I am capable of achieving the inconceivable and I will do the unimaginable." You are capable. Dictionary.com says that capable means having power and ability, efficient, competent1. Philippians 4:13 says, "I can do all things through Christ who strengthens me." In Christ, you have the power to do anything. You have the power to command a shift in your situation. You are not helpless. You are not hopeless in Christ. The Bible says in Matthew 19:26, "With God, all things are possible." In Christ, you are capable of starting that business. In Christ, you are capable of writing that book. In Christ, you have the power and the ability to efficiently and effectively do that thing that your family said that you could never do. In Christ, you have the ability to break generational curses, break negative generational habits, and break generational stigmas. You are capable because in Christ, you have power and authority.

Prayer of Activation

Father God, in the Name of Jesus, I come against every spirit on assignment to stop Your plan for my life. I bind every generational spirit of hindrance, every spirit of lack, and every spirit sent from the enemy that has hindered me from going forth and starting that business, writing that book, accomplishing that assignment, or completing that task you have given me. Today Lord, I stand on Your truth that I am capable--the impossible is possible for me in Christ. I thank You Lord for the power and the authority that You have given me in Christ. Nothing is too hard, and I can do all things through Christ who gives me strength. Today Lord, by faith, I celebrate all my future accomplishments and achievements in advance. I thank You Lord for awakening the sleeping giant that is inside of me. And I decree and declare that I will be and do all that You have called me to be and do, because You said that I am capable. Thank You, Father. I declare it done and I seal this prayer in Jesus' Name. Amen.

Today I just want you to remember that the Bible says that you are capable. When the enemy comes into your ears and tells you anything that is contrary to that, remember what I said before: it's a lie. You are capable because your Father in heaven has said so.

Day

12

I AM WORTHY

"God commendeth His love towards us, in that, while we were yet sinners, Christ died for us (KJV)."
Romans 5:8

"For God so loved the world that He gave His only begotten Son, that whoever believes in Him should not perish but have everlasting life."
John 3:16

I want you to know that you are worthy. Yes, you are worthy. Say it to yourself: "I am worthy. I am worthy." Romans 5:8 says, "God commendeth His love towards us, in that, while we were yet sinners, Christ died for us (KJV)." You are worthy. John 3:16 further confirms, "For God so loved the world that He gave His only begotten Son, that whoever believes in Him should not perish but have everlasting life." Now that's true love. God loves you so much that He gave His Son to die for you because you are worth it. Your chance to have eternal life meant that His Son had to die, and God still said that you were worth it. That's how important you are and how significant your life is.

Right now, I want to speak to that woman who is battling with the spirit of suicide. The spirit of suicide comes in to make you think that you are not worthy. I want you to know that there is a God in heaven who created your life with an assignment, with an agenda, and with a purpose. Whatever test or trial you may be going through right now, know that the Bible says that it is, "not worthy to be compared to the glory which shall be revealed in us" (Romans 8:18). God has a plan—even for your test and your trial. You are worthy of living this life. You are worthy! Your life is worth living, and you are worth it. You are worth it. You are worth it!

God sent His Son to die because He loved you so much, in order for you to have everlasting life. The enemy has come in to make you think that it's over. I'm here to tell you today that is not the case. That God has a plan for your life, and it is good. Jeremiah 29:11 says, "For I know the thoughts I think toward you, says the Lord, thoughts of peace and not of evil, to give you a future and a hope." The end of this journey is good, the fight is already fought, and you already won. So don't be sidetracked or deceived by the lie that your life is not worth anything. You are valuable, you are worthy, and you have been brought with a price.

Prayer of Activation

Today I come before you, Father God, binding the spirit of suicide that tries to infiltrate my mind and torment me with the lie that my life is worth nothing. Today, every suicidal thought, unction, or desire must cease and desist from operating in my mind now in Jesus' Name. Amen. I am worth living because Christ died so that I can have life, and that more abundantly (John 10:10). Father, today I bind all feelings of inadequacy. I come out of agreement with that lie that I am not good enough. For You said in Genesis 1:27, that I am made in Your image and likeness. Therefore, I am more than enough.

Father, today I come out of agreement with that lie that I am not worthy of the best. Help me, Father, to break from the yoke of abusive relationships in my life in Jesus' Name. Amen. No longer shall I settle for the abuser, for I am worthy of having healthy relationships with men who would love, adore, and honor me. I am worthy of having healthy relationships with people who cherish me just as I am, and people who would add value to my life.

Father, right now I come against negative and unhealthy thinking or unhealthy thought patterns. I pray, Lord, that You will touch my heart and mind so that I shall resist every lie of the enemy. I bind the spirit of low self-esteem that comes in to tell me that I am worthless.

Father, I dismantle and uproot every plot of the enemy sent to discredit my worthiness in Jesus' Name, Amen. Lord, I thank You for sending Your only Son to die just for me. Therefore, I am worthy. Thank You Lord, because I am no longer bound to the lies that were spoken over my life that devalued my worthiness. I declare from this day forth that my identity is rooted in You and I shall no longer give ear to anything that is contrary. Thank You Lord—because the spirit of suicide, thoughts of inadequacy and unworthy thought patterns no longer have a hold on me for my mind is renewed and I have been liberated in Jesus' Name, Amen. Lord I thank you for the shift that has taken place in my mindset and I decree and declare that Satan's attempts over my life are deemed powerless now in the mighty Name of Jesus. Amen.

I dare you to be the best you. Change your relationships if they are not enhancing your life. Start that business that you have desired to launch for so long. Apply for that promotion. Get that beautiful home you always dreamed of living in and begin to live your best life. I want you to remember and never forget that you are worthy—because Christ died, just for you.

Day

13

I AM STRONG

"Finally, my brethren, be strong in the Lord and in the power of His might. Put on the whole armor of God, that you may be able to stand against the wiles of the devil."

Ephesians 6:10-11

"I am strong. I am strong in the Lord. I am bold. I am courageous. I am daring. I am Strong." Ephesians 6:10 says, "Finally, my brethren, be strong in the Lord and in the power of His might. Put on the whole armor of God, that you may be able to stand against the wiles of the devil." The

Bible also says in verse 12, "For we do not wrestle against flesh or blood, but against principalities, against powers." That chapter goes on to break down the types of warfare that we as humans and believers will encounter in this life.

God has given you power and authority, but here's the amazing thing about God: He has given us all this power and authority, but we can go before the Father, and He will fight for us. But we have to make sure that we have on the armor of God. "Stand therefore, having girded your waist with truth, having put on the breastplate of righteousness, and having shod your feet with the preparation of the gospel of peace; above all, taking the shield of faith with which you will be able to quench all the fiery darts of the wicked one. And take the helmet of salvation, and the sword of the Spirit, which is the word of God..." (Ephesians 6: 14-17).

We have to cover ourselves. We have to gird ourselves. We have to protect ourselves, so that when the enemy comes (because he will come), we will be armored, protected, and covered by the Word of God. It is the Word that gives us the strength to endure. The Word of God is that very thing on the inside of us that keeps us moving forward and keeps us going onward. You are stronger than you think. Don't allow the enemy to lie to you and say that you are weak. You are stronger than you think because you have the full armor of God covering and protecting you.

So today repeat after me: I am strong. Yes, you are strong because the armor of the Most High God surrounds you. God has dispatched His angels to protect you wherever you go. Therefore, you are blessed, you are covered, you are anointed, and you are stronger than you think.

Prayer of Activation

Father God, today I nail to the Cross of Calvary every lie that I might have come into agreement with which says that I am not strong enough, that I can't do it, that I can't make it, or that this burden is too much to bear and this weight is too heavy for me to carry. I thank You Lord, because You said in Your Word that You won't give me more than I can bear. So Father, today and from this day forth, I put on the full armor of God so that I might be able to stand against the devices of Satan. Lord, I put on Your Word so that I might be able to repel every lie that may come my way. Today Lord, I stand in my Kingdom authority and I dispel every lie that has been spoken over my life. The Bible says in 2 Corinthians 4:8-9 that, "we are hard pressed on every side but not crushed; we are perplexed but not in despair; persecuted, but not abandoned; struck down but not destroyed." Father, I thank You that I am stronger than I realize because I have the power of Jesus Christ working on the inside of me. God, thank You for Your Word, which gives me the strength to endure. I seal this prayer in the mighty Name of Jesus. Amen.

Today I want you to meditate on God's truth: you are strong. No matter what comes your way, don't allow how you are feeling in the moment to deceive you. Remember that you are strong in the Lord and in the power of His might. Gone are the days where you allowed weakness to rule your life. It is time for you to rise up and be the warrior that God has created you to be. You are strong.

I AM INCREDIBLE

"But as it is written, eyes have not seen, nor ear heard, nor have it entered into the heart of man the things which God has prepared for those who love Him."
1 Corinthians 2:9

Today I want you to know without a shadow of doubt that you are incredible. Repeat after me: "I am incredible." The Scripture declares in 1 Corinthians 2:9, "But as it is written, eyes have not seen, nor ear heard, nor have it entered into the heart of man the things which God has prepared for those who love Him." You are incredible, and humanity has not scratched the surface of the things which God has in store for you.

I need you to really understand what incredible means. According to Lexico.com, here are some synonyms for the word incredible: magnificent, wonderful, marvelous, spectacular, remarkable, phenomenal, breathtaking, extraordinary, unbelievable, amazing, stunning, astounding, astonishing, inspiring, staggering, impressive, supreme, great, awesome1. You are incredible! This is who you are. This is who God created you to be: nothing less than the best. You are magnificent. You are astounding. You are astonishing. You are incredible. I encourage you to speak that, live that, and walk in that truth: you are incredible. The Creator of heaven and earth, the Creator of all that is seen and unseen has given you the keys to the Kingdom. He has given you all power and authority to fulfill His amazing purpose for your life and no one else can execute it as efficient as you. It is all in your hands. Therefore, nothing is too hard for you because you have the King of all kings and the Lord of all lords on your side. So today, I need you to overcome that fear and go for that promotion, start that business, create that invention, and start that program— because you are incredible.

Prayer of Activation

Father, in the Name of Jesus, I come before You today to take a moment to celebrate me: Your remarkable, inspiring, stunning, one-of-a-kind creation. I thank You Lord because I will live up to the very standard that You have set before me. I decree and declare that none of my dreams and desires will fall to the wayside, but I shall accomplish them all. I come against every lie that has been spoken against my identity and made me feel less that incredible. From this day forth, I declare: my latter days will be greater than the former days because I know who I am. I thank You Lord that everything that I desire according to Your will shall be released into my life now in the Name of Jesus. Today I declare that I, [Your Full Name], am extraordinary spectacular, remarkable, phenomenal, breathtaking, unbelievable, amazing, stunning, astounding, astonishing, inspiring, staggering, impressive, and incredible. Father, I worship and I praise You and I seal this prayer in Jesus' Name. Amen.

Remember, you're incredible. You're incredible. You are incredible! Begin to dispel every lie that is contrary to this truth and allow your new reality to influence how you show up in every area of your life.

Day 15

I AM REMARKABLE

"And she brought forth her firstborn Son, and wrapped Him in swaddling clothes, and laid Him in a manger, because there was no room for them in the inn."
Luke 2:7

"For there is born to you this day in the city of David a Savior, who is Christ the Lord, and this will be the sign to you: You will find a Babe wrapped in swaddling cloths, lying in a manger."
Luke 2:11-12

Repeat after me: "I am exceptional! I am sensational! I am outstanding! And I am remarkable in every single thing that I do." Make sure you are journaling this process, because God has already been ministering to your heart and I want you to see the transformation that has already been taking place within you. Today, however, I want you to meditate on the fact that you are absolutely remarkable. Dictionary. com defines remarkable as worthy of notice, or attention1. Luke 2:7,11-12 says, "And she brought forth her firstborn Son, and wrapped Him in swaddling clothes, and laid Him in a manger, because there was no room for them in the inn… For there is born to you this day in the city of David a Savior, who is Christ the Lord, and this will be the sign to you. You will find a Babe wrapped in swaddling cloths, lying in a manger." The cards that you were dealt in life does not determine your future. The King of kings and the Lord of lords—Jesus Christ, our Lord and Savior—was born in a manger, in the lowliest of situations. You need to understand that your start does not determine your end. God has a plan for your life, and it is greater than your beginning. Therefore, it's time for you to allow the truth of who God says that you are to stand up as a reality in your life.

Regardless of the situation, whether you were homeless or born to parents who were addicted to drugs, or any type of substance—whether you were neglected and had to go into the foster care or adoption system, or whatever the situation might have been, you have to know that Jesus Christ, our Lord and Savior, the King of all kings was born in a manger, surrounded by animals. I could just imagine the situation: it didn't smell good, it wasn't the warmest place, and it definitely wasn't the most sanitary environment. But the greatest Man that ever walked the face of this earth came from what seemed like nothing. And if you can relate—if your story parallels with that—I just want to encourage you and let you know that you are exceptional and sensational. You are remarkable in every single thing that you do. Just like our Lord and Savior, God has a plan for your life, and it is greater than your beginning.

Prayer of Activation

Lord, I come before You today to just say thank You. I thank You Lord for creating me and making me remarkable. You made my life to be worthy of notice and attention. And like Christ, regardless of my start, I know what You said in Romans 8:28, "And we know that all things work together for good to those who love God, to those who are the called according to His purpose." So today, I worship You, I honor You, and I glorify Your Holy Name because I now know that the plans that You have for my life are good. I know that my outcome is already good, even if I was dealt a bad hand in life. Father, You will be glorified through my story. So I thank You Lord for the test. I pray that if there is any area in my life that is not outstanding, remarkable or worthy of notice, that You are turning it around for my good and You are lining it up with Your perfect will for my life. Father, I just thank You and praise You because I have victory over the enemy. That situation does not determine my destiny because You already created a greater plan for my life, and it is remarkable. I seal this prayer in Jesus' Name. Amen.

I just want you to remember that that you are remarkable! Just like Christ, His beginning didn't determine His end. He now sits at the right hand of the Father and just like Christ, you are remarkable. Your life, your existence, your thoughts, and your ideas are worthy of notice and attention.

Day
16

I AM HEALED

"But He was wounded for our transgressions, He was bruised for our iniquities; the chastisement of our peace was upon Him, and by His stripes, we are healed."
Isaiah 53:5

Today I want you to step out on faith and I dare you to believe God for your healing. Whether it is for you, or you are standing in proxy for a friend or a loved one, I want you to activate your faith and declare that, "I [Name Here] am healed." I want to encourage you, stand in agreement with you, and remind you that you are healed. I need you to receive that in your spirit so that it can manifest in your body: you are healed! Repeat after me: "I am healed and I am in optimal health, perfect in every way from the crown of my head to the soles of my feet, I am healed, in Jesus' Name. Amen." I need you to receive that. Isaiah 53:5 says, "But He was wounded for our transgressions, He was bruised for our iniquities; the chastisement of our peace was upon Him, and by His stripes, we are healed." In Jesus' Name, you are healed of every wound, infirmity, sickness, disease, or anything else that the enemy has used to try to destroy you. I need you to know without a shadow of doubt that you are healed in the Name of Jesus.

Mark 11:23 boldly declares that, "...whoever says to this mountain, 'Be removed and be cast into the sea,' and does not doubt in his heart, but believes that those things he says will be done, he will have whatever he says." Based on this scripture, I want you to do whatever you have to do to build up your faith so that you can walk in the manifestation of total healing. You can read or listen to Scriptures about healing daily until your faith gets to a place where you are fully persuaded that you can be made whole through the Blood of Jesus. The Bible also declares in Isaiah 54:17 that, "no weapon formed against you shall prosper." That means that sickness, infirmity, or physical conditions cannot and will not harm you. Whatever the doctor's report may be, in Christ, you have the final say. Just know that the Word declares that by His stripes, you were healed. So today, I want you to begin to declare over your body, your mind—or whatever it is that is out of alignment with God's perfect will for your life—that you are healed in the name of Jesus. The Bible has given us power and authority—open your mouth and begin to command your healing to be made manifest in your life.

Prayer of Activation

Father, in the Name of Jesus, I come humbly before Your throne interceding for total healing and restoration in my mind and body. Father, You are a healer and a deliverer, and You make all things new. Today, I command ministering angels to be released to deliver miracles in my life now, in Jesus' Name, Amen. Father, I bind cancer, Crohn's disease, spinal diseases, psychological disorders, diabetes, sicknesses, any form of infirmity, and I command healing to be released now in my life in the Name of Jesus Christ, Amen. Father, I come against every spirit of infirmity that has come to keep me bound and I decree that it is by Your stripes that I am healed. Lord, it is by Your stripes that I have been liberated from the bondage of sickness and disease and I command its symptoms and its side effects, to go back to the pit of hell from where they came. I thank You Lord for total manifestation now in Jesus' Name. I stand by faith and I am fully persuaded that I am totally restored to optimal health in Jesus' Name. Amen. Father, I thank You for healing me from the crown of my head to the soles of my feet and I declare it done in Jesus' Name, Amen.

If you have not seen a "right now" manifestation, I want to encourage you and let you know that it is on the way. Because by His stripes, you were healed. So remember, throughout this day, begin to declare and command your healing to be manifested in your life. Continue to declare that you are healed in Jesus' Name, Amen.

Day
17

I AM AN OVERCOMER

"And they overcame him by the blood of the Lamb, and by the word of their testimony, and they did not love their lives to the death."
Revelations 12:11

I want to congratulate you on stepping out by faith and facing the giants that have kept you bound for so long. If you have made it this far, I believe without a shadow of doubt that you are being transformed into the greater and more powerful woman that God has created you to be.

The journey was not easy, and you could have quit a long time ago. But you are still standing. Therefore, you are an overcomer.

Repeat after me: "I am an overcomer. I have conquered through the blood of Christ. The word of my testimony is evidence that I am resolute in the faith, even when faced with death. Therefore, I am unstoppable. I am victorious. I won!" Revelations 12:11 says, "And they overcame him by the blood of the Lamb, and by the word of their testimony, and they did not love their lives to the death." The Bible declares in Proverbs 18:21 that, "Death and life are in the power of the tongue." It's time for you to speak over every dead situation in your life, because God has given you power. Job 22:28 says, "You will also declare a thing, and it will be established for you." No longer should you lie in defeat to the storms that the enemy sends your way. But now you have to activate the power and the authority that's already within you and overcome every obstacle by the words that you speak out of your mouth. God has given you so much power over that situation. You are no longer a victim in Christ because He has given you power to overcome every situation through the words that you declare. It is time for you to decree and declare the perfect will of God and command things to begin to shift in your favor.

Prayer of Activation

Lord, author and the finisher of my faith, I thank You, I worship You and glorify Your Holy and Matchless Name. Father, You have given me power and authority over every situation and over every obstacle that stands in my way. Father, You even instructed in Your Word that I should speak to the mountain and command it to be moved and cast into the sea—and if I have faith and do not doubt, it shall be done. Lord, You also said in Revelation 12:11, "And they overcame him by the blood of the Lamb, and by the word of their testimony, and they did not love their lives to the death." Lord, Your Word continues to affirm that I am an overcomer and I am victorious through Christ Jesus. Therefore, I am no longer a victim to the circumstances in my life that once held me down or tormented my mind. I am liberated by the blood of Jesus because I know that the fight is fixed, and in the end, it is good. Father, I worship You and I thank You that the battle is won, and I have overcome. Thank You Father for giving me victory over every situation and circumstance. I thank You that every obstacle has been moved out of my way. Lord, I thank You today for opening doors that no man can shut. I thank You for turning it around for my good. And I seal this prayer in Jesus' Name. Amen.

So today, I need you to remember, understand, and continue to celebrate because you are an overcomer in Christ Jesus. Even death cannot stop you. You are an overcomer.

Day 18

I AM ONE OF A KIND

"There's no one like her on earth, never has been, never will be. She's a woman beyond compare (MSG)."
Song of Solomon 6:9

Did you know that you are one of a kind? Yes, you are one of a kind. Repeat after me: "I am one of a kind. I am unique in every way. There's no one as amazing as me. I am transforming history. The one-of-a-kind me is impacting society." You are one of a kind! According to Dictionary. com, a synonym of one of a kind, is unique1. Song of

Solomon 6:9 goes on to describe you, and says that, "There's no one like her on earth, never has been, never will be. She's a woman beyond compare (MSG)." The King of all kings and the Lord of all lords says that there will never be a woman that will ever touch the face of this earth that will be like you, that will be as exceptional as you, as unique as you, as intelligent as you, as funny as you, as peculiar as you. How amazing is that?

Today, I want to encourage you to just be the outstanding, one-of-a-kind woman, that God created you to be. Don't try to change yourself to look like someone else, to be like someone else, or to act like someone else. God made you the way He made you for a reason. Why? Because He has given you a unique assignment on the Earth and it's going to transform lives. It is going to be a major blessing to other people. That is why it's so important that you stay the course and be who God created you to be. Remember, the enemy comes in to steal, kill and destroy your identity (John 10:10). His assignment is to make you think that there's nothing special about you. But that is a lie, because the Word says that there is no one on earth like you; there never has been, and never will be.

Prayer of Activation

Father, I come before You today taking a moment to celebrate my life, my purpose and my great destiny. Thank You Lord for making me unique in every way from the crown of my head to the soles of my feet. Today I rebuke every lie that the enemy has spoken into my life, and I repent for coming into agreement with them. Today, I declare Song of Solomon 6:9 over my life: I am beyond compare and there's no one else on this earth like me. I thank You Lord for the unique anointing that you have placed within me—to impact nations, transform societies, and to leave a legacy for generations to come. Thank You, Father for lighting the fire under me so that I might do something astonishing with my life. Today I celebrate my life and I decree and declare that I am a unique, one-of-a-kind gift to mankind, created to do great and marvelous works to the Glory of God. Father, I thank You and I praise You and I seal this prayer in Jesus' Name, Amen.

I want you to remember that you are one of a kind. There is no one on this earth like you, no one will ever touch this earth that will be like you. Therefore, let no one diminish your uniqueness or the authentic characteristics that God has created in you. Remember, you are one of a kind.

Day
19

I AM VIRTUOUS

"Who can find a virtuous woman?
or her price is far above rubies."
Proverbs 31:10 (KJV)

You are virtuous. Repeat after me: "I am a woman of virtue. Virtuous woman, that's me. I am a wife and His favor is upon my life. I am a mother and my children called me blessed. I am an entrepreneur and my wealth extends to those who serve with me." Dictionary.com defines virtue as having moral excellence1. Proverbs 31:10 declares, "who can find a virtuous woman? for her price is far above rubies." It's time for you to stop settling for less. And it's time for you to receive all that God the Father has for you. Some of you are staying in positions at your job because you are comfortable. You're comfortable, but you're frustrated. It's because the virtue inside of you is crying out for something greater. Remember, your price is far above rubies.

There are some of you who are staying in bad relationships, whether it's abusive or controlling, because you don't want to be alone. I need you to open your eyes and really see that he's not faithful and he doesn't respect you. I need you to know that God loves you as the queen that you are, and your price is far above rubies. You are not subpar, you are not less-than, and you are not worthless. Actually, the Bible describes you as a woman of great value and worth.

Prayer of Activation

I denounce every word-curse that was ever spoken over my life that told me that I was less than. I denounce every lie that causes me to act out of character or accept anything less than the best. I decree and declare that I am beginning to walk in my position as a virtuous woman. I command blessings upon blessings to locate me as I begin to walk in my divinely ordained authority as a woman of virtue. I bind every spirit that comes to derail or rob me of my identity, and I bind every spirit that comes to tell me that I am less than. I bind every lie that has been spoken over my life, and I uproot its effect now in the Name of Jesus. I commend every blessing that is assigned me to be released now, in the Name of Jesus. Amen.

I want you to remember and get it in your spirit: you are a woman of virtue. You are a woman of great value. And a woman of great worth. You are virtuous!

Day

20

I AM FORGIVEN

*"Therefore if anyone is in Christ, he is a new creation. Old
things have passed away, and behold,
all things have become new."*
2 Corinthians 5:17

Daughter, you are forgiven. I need you to repeat after me
and say: "I am forgiven! Yes, I am forgiven!" I need you to
receive that. 2 Corinthians 5:17 says, "Therefore if anyone is
in Christ, he is a new creation. Old things have passed away,
and behold, all things have become new." Today, I need you

to get it in your spirit that you are forgiven. Christ paid the price of every sin that was ever committed—past, present, and future. You have been redeemed by the Blood of Jesus Christ. Therefore, there are no more chains holding you. In Christ, you have been justified by faith, with justified meaning "made right." So if your family, your friends, or even you yourself are still condemning you for something you did in the past, I want you to know that today, as long as you repent, you are forgiven.

There are also people who have wronged you. There are people who have taken advantage of you. There are people who have misused, neglected, and rejected you. Today, I encourage you to release them. Forgive them so that you can receive all that God has for you.

Now, let's take a moment to reflect on anyone who has ever wronged you in any way. Pause for a few minutes and begin to think. Allow the Holy Spirit to bring them back to your memory. I want you to grab a sheet of paper and begin to write down their names. Please take some time to do this; don't rush the process. The Lord wants you to be free and whole.

Next, I want you to think about those involved in any of your childhood trauma. You want to make sure you put them on the list. Think about people who have wronged you in any way in your teenage years, even in adulthood.

Think about the people who have abandoned or rejected you. Think about the friends who betrayed you. Add these people to your list and don't rush through this.

Now that your list is complete, I'm going to walk you through a forgiveness prayer. Repeat after me. "I [your name], forgive [the person's name], for the offense of [name the offense] which they committed against me." You will want to write out what that offense was. I know for many of you, this is not easy at all. I pray that the peace of God comforts you and gives you strength. Some of the things that you have gone through have been very traumatic and mind blowing. But again, I pray that the Holy Spirit will come in and give you the grace you need to walk through this process of total healing and deliverance. I want you to do this for every single person who you have listed on your sheet of paper.

Make sure that you connect your heart with the words that you speak. You're not just reading words from a piece of paper. You're doing this from the very depths of your heart, because you have to know and understand that forgiveness is for you, to set you free, to release the venom that you've been holding in. Here is an example: Susan is forgiving her ex-husband, Larry: "I, Susan Smith, forgive my ex-husband, Larry Smith, for infidelity and for betraying my trust—for making me feel less than worthy as a woman and for destroying our family." I use this as an example to help guide you. Now, plug in your situation and your offenders and break it down that way. I encourage you to take as much time as you need to complete this process.

I know that this may not have been an easy process for you, but I want to encourage you and let you know that on the other side of this is liberty. On the other side of this is blessing, on the other side of this is healing and freedom. Remember, forgiveness is for you.

If you feel like you are truly ready to take the next step and really release your offenders from your heart, take that piece of paper and begin to rip it up. As you rip that paper, it is a symbol of you releasing that person. It's a symbol of you releasing those people who betrayed you, offended you, abandoned you, abused you, and rejected you. And this begins the process of your healing and your deliverance. Hallelujah! I am so proud of you and I am excited for you. The enemy had you imprisoned in the memory of your trauma, but today I decree by faith that you are liberated. NO MORE CHAINS HOLDING YOU! I encourage you to pause and take a moment to worship the Lord for this bold step that you made today!

Prayer of Activation

Father God, in the mighty and matchless Name of Jesus, I come before You Lord, thanking you for setting me free from the shackles of my past. Father, today I took a bold leap of faith and forgave those who have wronged me. Lord, I pray that you will release Your peace within me, in Jesus' Name. Amen. Father, I command ministering angels to be released right now to cover and strengthen me. Help me Father, as I have made the decision to let go of the past, let go of the hurt, let go of the shame and forgive myself and my offenders. Father God I thank You that Your Word declares, "Whom the Son sets free is free indeed." So on this day, [fill in today's day, month, and year], I have been liberated from those memories that once had me bound. Lord, I celebrate that today marks the beginning of the rest of my life. No longer shall I be bound by the bitter root of unforgiveness. No longer shall my body be plagued with the effects of unforgiveness. Today I decree and declare that I am no longer bound to the offenses that have once affected my life. Today I declare that I am free, and I am liberated. Hallelujah! I decree and declare that as I stepped out by faith and forgave my offenders, You restored, renewed, and revived me. Father, I thank You for new beginnings being released in my life today. I thank You for healing being released in my life today. I thank You Lord for deliverance manifesting in my life today. I thank You because every blessing that was held up as a result of my unforgiveness is now being released! Hallelujah.

Father, I bless You and I praise You. I thank You for Your healing power. I thank You for Your restoration of power. I thank You, for Your glory has been released in my life today. I seal this prayer in the mighty Name of Jesus, and I decree and declare that if there are any demonic messengers listening in on this prayer, that they are deemed powerless now in the Name of Jesus. Amen. Father, I thank You that this prayer, along with every request made today, is piercing through the heavenlies and entering into Your throne room, Lord. Father, I seal this prayer in Your Blood, in Jesus' Name. Amen.

Now I must warn you, the enemy will try to come back and use that same person—or someone else—to harm you in the same way or a similar way. But you must recognize that this is a blatant attack from the enemy against your deliverance in that area.

Secondly, you need to remember that you have been released; you have been liberated from that offense. Now, you must begin to speak over your heart and your mind so that you will not go back to that place of hurt, or that place of isolation.

And thirdly, you must pray. You have to continue to intercede and continue to pray for God to turn away the enemy. God promises in Malachi 3:11 that, "I will rebuke the devourer for your sakes." You must begin to speak over your situation and decree and declare the perfect will of God for your life and command victory to be your portion.

Remember, from this day forth, you are a new creation in Christ Jesus. When the Father looks upon you, He no longer sees your sin. He no longer sees the offense. He only sees the Blood of Jesus. Therefore, you are forgiven. Thank You, Lord.

Day
21

I AM WHOLE

*"Now may the God of peace Himself sanctify you completely;
and may your whole spirit, soul, and body be preserved
blameless at the coming of our Lord Jesus Christ."*
1 Thessalonians 5:23

You are whole. Repeat after me: "I am whole. I am physically, psychologically, socially, spiritually, and financially whole in Jesus' Name. Amen." 1 Thessalonians 5:23 says, "Now may the God of peace Himself sanctify you completely; and may your whole spirit, soul, and body be preserved blameless at the coming of our Lord Jesus Christ." In John 5:6 (King James Version), Jesus asks a question to the lame man who sat waiting to be carried to the pool of Bethesda. He asked him, "Wilt thou be made whole?" This man had a decision to make: did he want to stay in his current state? Or did he want everything that God had for him: the ability to walk and to be free? So, I ask you this question today: will thou be made whole? Are you ready to walk in wholeness? Are you ready to live in the fulfillment of living a life for Christ?

When you live for Christ, nothing can stand against you. Nothing in your life will be lacking; nothing will be missing. Today, I really want to challenge you to live a life where you will be blameless before the Father. It is a life where you will be whole, with nothing missing and nothing lacking. I am talking about being emotionally whole in the way you look at yourself, and whole in the thoughts that you think about yourself. That's wholeness. Are you ready to get to a place where you are socially whole? That means surrounding yourself with people who will build you up, edify you, and stretch you to be greater and be better. Are you ready to be to be spiritually whole? That means receiving all the blessings that God has for you. Having an intimate relationship with the Lord. Are you ready to be financially whole? That means never lacking, and always operating in increase, prosperity, and abundance. God wants you to be whole—in every area, every aspect, every facet of your life. Now is the time for you to walk in it. Just like Jesus asked the lame man in John chapter 5: "Wilt thou be made whole?"

The Father is asking you, "Daughter, are you ready to live life? Are you ready to live again? Are you ready to breathe again? Are you ready to be healed? Are you ready to be well in every area of your life? Are you ready to be made whole?"

Prayer of Activation

Father, I come before You, praying that You would touch me in every area of my life that is missing, where there is brokenness, or where I am lacking. Lord, I pray that You would make me whole emotionally. I pray God that You will open my eyes so that I will see that I am made in Your image and likeness. I pray that You will shift my perspective so that I see that I am fearfully and wonderfully made.

Father breathe on my finances. I command increase and overflow to begin to locate me from the North, the South, the East, and the West. I bind lack and mediocracy, and I command increase to be my portion from this day forth.

Father, I pray for my health. I bind up every spirit of sickness, disease, and infirmity in Jesus' Name. Amen. I decree and declare that from the crown of my head to the soles of my feet that I am divinely well, and every aspect of my body is lining up to Your perfect will for its natural function. Lord, I thank You, and I believe by faith according to Isaiah 53:5, that physically I am whole in Jesus' Name. Amen.

Father, I thank You for making me whole in every way—mind, body, and spirit—so that I may be kept blameless according to 1 Thessalonians 5:23. I thank You for total wholeness, spiritually and in every area of my life. I decree and declare that I will walk in the fullness of who You have called me to be, so that lives will be transformed, and souls be delivered. Father, I thank You and I seal this prayer in Jesus' Name. Amen.

Remember, in Christ, you have already been made whole, nothing missing, nothing broken. You are whole!

Day
22

I AM FAVORED

*"So shalt thou find favour and good understanding in the
sight of God and man (KJV)."*
Proverbs 3:4

Today I want you to know that you are favored by the Most
High God. Repeat after me: "I am favored by God and
man. Everywhere I go, blessings upon blessings overtake
me. Doors supernaturally open for me and unexpected favor
is granted to me." Proverbs 3:4 says, "So shalt thou find
favour and good understanding in the sight of God and
man (KJV)." When you're favored by God, then favor from

man follows. According to Dictionary.com, favor is defined as excessive kindness from a place of goodwill1. God will open doors for you that no man can shut. He will cause companies to adjust their policies to accommodate you. He will cause you to get a raise on just your second day on the job. He will cause things to shift and turn around for your benefit. He will cause bills that were due to supernaturally disappear. Now that's what I call the Favor of God!

Are you ready to walk in the favor that God has for you, His daughter? That's the posture that you need to have everywhere you go and in everything you do. Because of the favor of God on your life, things will shift and swing in your favor. Even if you don't feel that you deserve it, God does. He will open doors for you because He has a plan and an assignment for you to fulfill. Favor will make a way out of no way, so that you can go forth and do what God is calling you to do.

Today, I challenge you to begin to walk with the posture, the boldness and the confidence of knowing that you are a favored daughter of the Most High God. The King of all kings, the Lord over all lords has granted you favor and has given you special approval: the VIP access. When you go through life knowing that you are chosen by God—that you've been sent and set apart and have been favored by God—then nothing (and I mean nothing) should stop you. When you shift your perspective and see yourself as the daughter of the King of kings, you will begin to attract the blessings that God has for you. Doors will begin to supernaturally open for you because the hand of God is orchestrating and moving things in your favor.

Prayer of Activation

Father, I come before You, thanking You for bestowing Your favor upon my life. I pray that everywhere I go, Your glory will rest upon me and doors will open for me that no man can shut. Lord, I pray that businesses, organizations, and institutions will adjust their policies to accommodate my divine assignment in Jesus' Name. Amen. I thank You for crowning me with favor and glory. I decree and declare that in this season, I will begin to see myself the way You see me Lord, so that I will receive every blessing that You have for me. Father, I come against every lie and trick of the enemy, every snare and every trap set by the enemy, to make me think that I am not favored or worthy. Father, thank You for delivering me from the many lies and curses that has been spoken over my life. I decree and declare from this day forth that I shall walk in the power, the authority, and the anointing of a favored woman of God. I declare that it is done. I seal this prayer in Jesus' Name. Amen.

Remember, you are favored by God. Everywhere you go, and in everything you do, the favor of God rests upon you. So begin to receive the benefits of being God's favored daughter.

Day

23

I AM PROSPEROUS

"Surely goodness and mercy shall follow me All the days of my life and I will dwell in the house of the LORD Forever."
Psalms 23:6

"But my God shall supply all of your needs according to His riches in glory by Christ Jesus."
Philippians 4:19

You are prosperous. Repeat after me: "I am prosperous. I am the pitcher of divine wealth. Everything I touch prospers." Psalms 23:6 says, "Surely goodness and mercy shall follow me All the days of my life and I will dwell in the house of the LORD Forever." The Bible also says in Philippians 4:19, "But my God shall supply all of your needs according to His riches in glory by Christ Jesus." In Christ, you are prosperous. Only goodness and mercy shall follow you all the days of your life. In Christ, every need in your life is met.

If you have a need in your life right now, I need you to go before God and begin to make your request known. The Bible says, "Ask, and it shall be given you (KJV)" (Matthew 7:7). The Bible also says, "Give, and it shall be given unto you: good measure, pressed down, shaken together, and running over (KJV)" (Luke 6:38a). When God talks about prosperity, He's not just talking financially. He's talking about emotional prosperity, spiritual prosperity, financial prosperity, and psychological prosperity. God wants you to be prosperous in every area of your life.

It is time for the spirit of lack to be broken off your life and the windows of heaven to be opened for you. God has a storehouse full of blessings with your name on it. Now is the time for you to ask the Holy Spirit for strategy to release it into your hands. James 2:26b says, "Faith without works is dead." You must act upon the idea or instructions that the Lord has given you to release wealth and resources into your hands. Remember, your breakthrough is dependent on you stepping out by faith and acting on the instructions released to you. That business, that promotion, that new home, that new vehicle, your peace of mind, good health, and so much more is waiting for you. It's yours. Go and get it. You are prosperous!

Prayer of Activation

Father, I come before You right now and I speak breakthrough over every area of my life. Where there is lack, I command increase to overtake me. Where there is sickness, I command health to be my portion. Where there is sorrow, let peace and joy invade the atmosphere of my environment. I command that, "goodness and mercy shall follow me all the days of my life," according to Psalm 23:6. In the name of Jesus, I decree and declare that I am walking into my season of unmerited prosperity. I command the windows of heaven to open up for me and I declare that everything I touch prospers. I declare that every place that the sole of my feet threads upon is blessed in Jesus Name, Amen. I thank you, Lord that this is my season of increase— this is my season of overflow and miracles shall find me everywhere I go and in everything that I do. Therefore, I am abundantly blessed and prosperous in Jesus Name, Amen.

It is time for you to work and celebrate because your latter will be greater than your former. I need you to remember this. I need you to jump for joy because you are prosperous. If you are lacking in your finances, your health, or your relationships, begin to create plan of action and then celebrate because you are prosperous. Declare it until God's promises are released into your life. Remember, you are prosperous because God says so. Amen.

Day

24

I AM COMPLETE

"You are complete in Him, who is the head of
all principality and power."
Colossians 2:10

Today I want you to know that you are complete. Repeat after me: "I am complete!" Colossians 2:10 says, "You are complete in Him, who is the head of all principality and power." In this text, complete in the Greek is pléroó, meaning fulfilled, finished, and accomplished1. When you made the decision to give your life to Christ, your life became fulfilled. Your purpose was finished, and everything you set your mind to do was accomplished in Christ. I want to encourage you to stay the course. Don't quit because it is hard. Don't quit even though you don't see a way out—because out of no way, a way will be made.

Be encouraged, because God will put His stamp of completion upon every plan that you have for your life, as long as it lines up with the Word. Regardless of the obstacles that may come your way—or the things that the enemy sends to set you back and derail you—as long as you stay the course, everything that you set your mind to do will be fulfilled. It will be finished. It will be accomplished. It will be complete in Christ and you will have the victory.

Prayer of Activation

Father, I thank You because I am complete in You and fulfilled in every area of my life. I thank You, knowing that I will finish every assignment and accomplish every task that You have for me. Lord, I decree and declare that I will stay the course and complete everything that I have set my heart and mind to do. Father, I command every demonic spirit on assignment to derail me to cease and desist from their activities in Jesus' Name. Amen. I decree and declare that I am developing spiritual stature through Christ Jesus, and nothing in my life is missing or broken. I thank You, Father, because I walk in the benefits of being complete in You. Therefore, doors are opening for me that no man can shut. Lord, thank You for crowning me with favor and glory everywhere that I go. Thank You Lord—every task that You have given me, I shall see it to the end. Nothing shall by any means stop me. Father, I thank You for blessing, keeping, and covering me as I live for You. I seal this prayer in Jesus' Name. Amen.

I just want you to remember that you are complete, and you are developing spiritual stature through Christ's will, for He is the head and rule over all authority and angelic power in the earth. Therefore, in Christ, you are complete, lacking nothing. Be encouraged.

Day
25

I AM FASCINATING

דד

*"And Barak called Zebulun and Naphtali to Kadesh; he went
up with ten thousand men under his command, and Deborah
went up with him."*
¬Judges 4:10

Today I want you to look in the mirror and ponder for a
moment on how fascinating you are. Repeat after me: "I am
fascinating. I am captivating. Everyone who knows me is
fascinated by my wisdom, my beauty, and my strength. Yes,

I am so fascinating." You are fascinating! Judges 4 tells the story of a great woman of God. Her name was Deborah. In verse 10, the Bible makes mention of her: "And Barak called Zebulun and Naphtali to Kadesh; he went up with ten thousand men under his command, and Deborah went up with him." Deborah was a woman of God who broke tradition. She was a woman of great wisdom. She was a fascinating woman. She had sound judgment. She was sought after. She was a prophetess and a war strategist. Actually, she was the only female judge during that time when women could not hold political positions. Now, that's fascinating!

In order for this great woman to defy the odds and break tradition, there had to be some type of warrior in her. She had to possess some type of tenacity. She had to have a level of determination to make her sought after, and the only woman eligible to stand with Barak and ten thousand men as they went into war. The reason I share her story is because in every one of you, there is a Deborah. There is a woman of great wisdom and judgment—that woman who has the ability to make keen decisions. There's a warrior on the inside of you. There's someone who is courageous and has the drive to do something outside of the norm. I need you to know today that you are fascinating; the world is in eager anticipation for your arrival. Now it is time for you to rise up, stand up, and go forth to do all that God has called you to do.

Prayer of Activation

Father, today in the Name of Jesus, I speak to the Deborah that is lying dormant inside of me. Father God, I call the warrior in me to come forth now in the Name of Jesus. Father, You created me to be a visionary, an innovator, a businesswoman, an entrepreneur, a doctor, a lawyer, a dancer, and so much more. Lord, You equipped me with fascinating abilities to confound the mind of man. Father, I pray that I will no longer be hindered by the lies that were spoken upon my character. Instead I will begin to stand on Your Word and operate in all that you have called me to do. I thank You Lord because the warrior in me is rising up and coming forth so that nations can be transformed, societies set free, and people restored and delivered. Father, thank You for what You are doing in my life. Just like Deborah, I will make an impact in my nation that will be the catalyst for radical change. Lord, I bless You and I praise You in Jesus' Name. Amen.

I need you to remember God's truth that you are captivating to everyone who knows you. They are fascinated by you. Therefore, I urge you to go forth without fear or reservation and allow the Lord to use you in the mightiest way.

I AM A CONQUEROR

*"Yet in all these things, we are more than conquerors
through Him who loved us."*
Romans 8:37

Did you know that you are a conqueror? Repeat after me: "I am a conqueror." The King James Version Dictionary defines conqueror as one who conquers, one who gains victory, or one who subdues and brings into subjection or possession by force or by influence1. Romans 8:37 says, "Yet in all these things, we are more than conquerors through

Him who loved us." The Bible further states in Matthew 11:12 that, "…the kingdom of heaven suffers violence, and the violent take it by force." God has given you power and authority to conquer and have dominion in every area of your life. If there is any area of your life that is out of order, it is time for you to take back your authority.

If your children are behaving out of order, it's time for you to begin to speak over their lives, take dominion, and stop the enemy from moving and operating in their lives. If your relationships are not in alignment with the Word of God, then you must take it by force. I'm not talking about physical force, because the Bible says in Ephesians 6:12 that, "For we wrestle not against flesh and blood, but against principalities, against powers, against the rulers of the darkness of this world, against spiritual wickedness in high places (KJV)." We need to fight through our words, our praise, and the Word of God. These are all weapons of warfare that we can use to violently defeat and destroy the enemy.

I need you to know that you are more than a conqueror in Christ Jesus. The Scriptures declare that Satan is defeated, and you have the victory. Therefore, it's time for you to stop allowing life to tell you who is boss and begin to take the authority that God has given you. Now is the time for you to begin to take dominion over every area of your life that is not in alignment with God's will for your life—because in Christ Jesus, you are more than a conqueror. In Christ Jesus, you have the victory. In Christ Jesus, you have the power to subdue and bring unto subjection anything that is not in alignment with the Word of God.

Prayer of Activation

Father, I thank You because in Romans 8:37, You declare that I am more than a conqueror in Christ Jesus. I thank You Lord, because Jesus died on the Cross—but on the third day, He rose again, taking the keys from death, hell and the grave. Therefore, Satan has no power or authority in my life. Father, I thank You because I am walking in the power and the authority that You have given me as a child of the Most High God. Thank You Lord for releasing divine strategy to violently take back my peace of mind and my joy. I thank You because I have control in my home, and my children are whole, obedient, and well behaved.

I thank You Father because I know who I am in You, and know the divine power that I operate in. Therefore, I decree and declare that Your perfect will be made manifest over my life, over my children's lives, over my marriage, over my finances, and over any area of my life that is not in alignment with you, Father. I thank You Lord for making me a conqueror in every area of my life. I have the victory now, in Jesus' Name. Amen.

Remember that you are a conqueror in Christ Jesus. Therefore, nothing can hold you down. Nothing can stop you. Nothing can take you out. Every promise that the Lord has given you is already yours, so go and get it! Now that you know who you are, the devil cannot stop you. In Christ, you are a conqueror. You have the victory, and you've already won. It is done in Jesus' Name. Amen.

Day
27

I AM BLESSED

"Now it shall come to pass, if you diligently obey the voice of the Lord your God, to observe carefully all His commandments which I command you today, that the Lord your God will set you high above all nations of the earth. And all these blessings shall come upon you and overtake you, because you obey the voice of the Lord your God: 'Blessed shall you be in the city, and blessed shall you be in the country. Blessed shall be the fruit of your body, the produce of your ground and the increase of your herds, the increase of your cattle and the offspring of your flocks. Blessed shall be your basket and your kneading bowl. Blessed shall you be when you come in, and blessed shall you be when you go out."

Deuteronomy 28:1-6

Did you know that you are blessed? I am talking to you. Yes, you are blessed! Repeat after me: "I am blessed! I am blessed in every way. I am blessed every day. I am blessed everywhere I go. I am blessed and everyone shall know. I am blessed! I am blessed! Yes, I am blessed."

Deuteronomy 28: 1-6 says, "Now it shall come to pass, if you diligently obey the voice of the Lord your God, to observe carefully all His commandments which I command you today, that the Lord your God will set you high above all nations of the earth. And all these blessings shall come upon you and overtake you, because you obey the voice of the Lord your God: 'Blessed shall you be in the city, and blessed shall you be in the country. Blessed shall be the fruit of your body, the produce of your ground and the increase of your herds, the increase of your cattle and the offspring of your flocks. Blessed shall be your basket and your kneading bowl. Blessed shall you be when you come in, and blessed shall you be when you go out," You are blessed in every way, you are blessed every day, and everything that you touch is blessed. Why? Because you are an obedient, faithful follower of your Lord and Savior, Jesus Christ. Whatever the Father tells you to do, do it because it will open the windows of heaven for you. Again, the Bible says in Deuteronomy 28:3 that you will be blessed in the city, and you will be blessed in your field. Then the scripture goes on to say that the "fruit of your body" (meaning your children) will be blessed. Everything you put your hands to will be blessed:

your livestock, your businesses, and everything else that you touch will be blessed when you obey the Lord.

I want to challenge you today: if there is something that the Lord is asking you to do, if it is outside of your comfort zone, or something that you don't feel qualified to do, I want to tell you today that the Lord qualifies you. Your obedience will unlock an avalanche of blessings to be released into your life. Just know that you are capable and that you are good enough. Go ahead and do that thing that He is calling you to do, so that you can be blessed and the lives of others can be transformed through your obedience.

Prayer of Activation

Father, I thank You that Your Word declares that I am blessed. Therefore, I command the blessings of Abraham to begin to locate me from the North, the South, the East, and the West. I pray, Father, that just like Abraham, You will make my name great and You will continue to open doors for me that no man can shut. I thank You Lord for making a way out of no way for me and turning things around for my good. Father, I thank You today for releasing Your blessings upon me because I obey your instructions and I submit to your Word.

Father, I command my blessings to flow, unhindered and uncontaminated in the Name of Jesus. Lord, I thank You for opening up the windows of heaven and pouring out a blessing that I won't even have room enough to receive. But I declare that in this season, Father, You are giving me new wine skins to handle the new level of anointing, the new level of overflow, and the new level of increase that you are releasing into my life. Lord, thank You—my life will never be the same.

Father, I thank You for overtaking me with blessings as You said in Your Word in Amos 9:13-15 (MSG): "Things are going to happen so fast your head will swim, one thing fast on the heels of the other. You won't be able to keep up. Everything will be happening at once—and everywhere you look, blessings! Blessings like wine pouring off the mountains and hills." Father, I just thank You for releasing Your blessings, Your increase, Your overflow, Your unmerited favor into my life and I thank You, Lord, that the devourer cannot, shall not and will not take what You are releasing to me. I decree and declare that my season of highs and lows or ups and downs are ending. From this moment forth, I am entering into a cycle of steady increase and overflow because I am blessed in the mighty Name of Jesus. Amen.

I want you to begin celebrating this next season of blessings—this avalanche of blessing that is coming your way today and every day. Even if the situation seems contrary, begin to prophesy to your situation and declare that, "I am blessed," because you really are blessed, and the Bible tells you so.

Day 28

I AM RIGHTEOUS

"The mouth of a righteous man is a well of life (KJV)."
Proverbs 10:11a

"The fruit of the righteous is a tree of life."
Proverbs 11:30a

You are righteous. Repeat after me: "I am righteous. I am the righteousness of God, created in Christ Jesus. I am established in the Kingdom of God. I am a joint heir to all its wealth. Therefore, I am righteous." Proverbs 10:11

says, "The mouth of a righteous man is a well of life," and Proverbs 11:30 says, "The fruit of the righteous is a tree of life." Thesaurus.com describes righteous as being good, virtuous, upright, upstanding, and moral1. When you think about a well, it is a structure created in the ground by digging and drilling deep into the earth to access water. The process and the trials that you have gone through in your life make up the excavation process that God has allowed you to endure to bring you to a place where the water from the well of life inside of you can pour out into the lives of the people that you have been called to reach. Of the trials that you've been through in your life, God has allowed every situation and circumstance to bring you to a place where your story will resurrect the dead and give hope to someone who is hopeless. Mighty woman of God, today I challenge you to go forth and do what God is calling you to do.

Proverbs 11:30 says, "The fruit of the righteous is a tree of life." When you look at a fruitful tree, you know that it doesn't feed only one person. It can feed a village. Just like the tree of life, your process, your story, and the fruit that comes from it can give life to the people who eat from that fruit. What do I mean by that? Whenever you tell your story of what God has brought you through, you are giving life to someone who feels hopeless. Whenever you testify about how God has made a way out of no way for you, the person who hears your story is eating the fruit from your tree. Therefore, your words are giving them life and hope that they can make it too.

Prayer of Activation

Father God, I come before You in the Name of Jesus, taking this moment to thank You for all that You have done for me. I am not worthy of every blessing that You have bestowed upon me. But today I worship You, I praise You, and I glorify You for sending Your Son Jesus to die on the Cross. Through His death and resurrection, I have been made righteous in Christ Jesus.

Father, I thank You for every test and trial that You have allowed me to go through. Lord, I thank You for giving me the strength to hold on during the difficult seasons in my life. Just like a well which had to be excavated, I had to go through the bending and breaking so that my anointing could flow, and so that I could be a well of life to those who connect with me. Father, I thank You because my testimony is now a well of life to those who drink of it.

Father, Your Word declares in Proverbs 11:30 that, "the fruit of the righteous is a tree of life." Lord, I thank You because my testimony is life to those who hear it. Just like a tree, my story will bear fruit. It will activate the giftings and the anointing that are lying dormant within someone's life. Lord, thank You because I am no longer bound, but set free in Jesus to do great and marvelous works. I thank You and I praise You. I seal this prayer in Jesus' Name, Amen.

Remember: you are righteous. You are virtuous. You are upstanding in the eyes of the Father. Your past does not determine your future. You have been justified by faith and you have been made righteous in Christ Jesus. So go forth and live. Be all that God has created you to be and do greater .Your story will be a radical blessing to all those who hear it.

Day

29

I AM ANOINTED

"But the anointing which you have received from Him abides in you, and you do not need that anyone teach you; but as the same anointing teaches you concerning all things, and is true, and is not a lie, and just as it has taught you, you will abide in Him."

1 John 2:27

Did you know that you are anointed? Repeat after me: "I am anointed. I am anointed by God. I am a recipient of His special gift that remains in me permanently. His anointing teaches me and gives me insight. Everywhere I go, the anointing upon my life causes supernatural experiences to happen to me. I am anointed." 1 John 2:27 says, "But the anointing which you have received from Him abides in you, and you do not need that anyone teach you; but as the same anointing teaches you concerning all things, and is true, and is not a lie, and just as it has taught you, you will abide in Him." In both 1 John 2 and Luke 4, we see that the Bible is talking about the Holy Spirit.

When you accepted Jesus Christ as your Lord and Savior, one of the very first gifts that you received was the gift of the Holy Spirit. He came into your heart to guide, direct and lead your life. The anointing that you carry is the Holy Spirit of God Himself, the third being in the Godhead, residing in you. You have all power and authority in your hands. Anything you need to know, the Holy Spirit will teach you. And He is not like man; He does not lie. The Holy Spirit gives you power and authority. Through the Holy Spirit, you can lay hands on the sick and see them recover. God has given you the Holy Spirit and through Him, you have the power, authority and anointing to go forth and do the will of the Father.

Today, I encourage you to go forth and do all that God has created you to do, because you are not alone on this journey. You have God Himself residing inside of you. Don't be moved by what your physical environment looks like, or by your temporary financial limitations. Don't be moved by what you don't have, including educational degrees or diplomas. If God has placed a vision in your heart, then you are equipped with everything that you need to bring it to pass. All you need is faith with a whole lot of work. Remember, the journey is not going to be easy. There are going to be a lot of obstacles in your way that will try to stop you. Don't quit! You are called and anointed for the assignment that the Lord has given you to fulfill. All you need to do is trust the leading of the Holy Spirit—that still, small voice—and move by faith. Then watch God blow your mind!

Prayer of Activation

Heavenly Father, I come before You today thanking You for seeing fit to dwell within me. Lord, I thank You for the Holy Spirit that intercedes for me, leading, guiding, covering, and protecting me. Most of all, Lord, I thank You for anointing me to go forth and to proclaim liberty to the captives, to preach the Gospel, to administer healing to the sick, and to proclaim life and victory over dead situations. Father, I thank You that I am anointed by You. And, I thank You that the Holy Spirit resides inside of me.

Lord, I thank You for the victory that is being released in every area of my life. I decree and declare that from this day forth, I shall walk in the power and authority of the anointing that resides inside me. Therefore Lord, if there is anything that I need, I can come boldly to Your throne and ask for it. I believe that You will release it to me according to Your will. Lord, I thank You that I am no longer bound by fear or doubt or feelings of inadequacy because my identity is rooted in you. Father, I thank You that I am not moved by my natural limitations because You are Jehovah Jireh—my Provider—and You shall supply all my needs according to Your riches in glory by Christ Jesus (Philippians 4:19 (KJV)). Father, I thank You for the Holy Spirit and I thank You for sending Your Son to die so that I might have life and have it more abundantly. Lord, I thank You, I praise You, and I seal this prayer in Jesus' Name. Amen.

Remember, you are anointed—not by man, but by God. Therefore, you have power. You have authority. You have victory in every situation. You are anointed.

I AM A MASTERPIECE

*"For you formed my inward parts; You covered me in
my mother's womb. I praise You, for I am fearfully and
wonderfully made; Marvelous are Your works, and that my
soul knows very well."*
Psalm 139:13–14

We are going to conclude these thirty days by declaring
that you are God's masterpiece. Repeat after me: "I am
God's masterpiece." Yes, you are God's masterpiece. You
are His work of art. I need you to know and understand

that God took His time when He intricately and uniquely wove you in your mother's womb. Psalm 139:13- 14 declares, "For you formed my inward parts; You covered me in my mother's womb. I praise You, for I am fearfully and wonderfully made; Marvelous are Your works, and that my soul knows very well." Webster's Dictionary defines masterpiece as a work done with extraordinary skill, or a supreme intellectual or artistic achievement1. I need you to understand that you are God's supreme achievement. When God created you, the Bible says in Psalms 139, that He formed your inward parts; He intricately woven you in your mother's womb. Intricately means that He was specific with every detail, and He didn't rush this process. God calls you a masterpiece, which is a supreme work of art done by a qualified craftsman.

When you think of a masterpiece, you may think of a work of art. When the Lord formed you and sculpted you, He gave you your hair color, eye color, and height. He endowed you with certain personality traits. He was not satisfied until He saw you as perfect. Just like a painting, every stroke and color serves its purpose. Every facet of your being has a purpose unto Christ Jesus.

Prayer of Activation

Father God, in the Name of Jesus— author and finisher of our faith, the ultimate architect, Jehovah Jireh, Jehovah Rapha, Alpha and Omega, the beginning and the end—Lord, I thank You for the transformation that I know has taken place in my life. At the beginning of this journey, I had a tainted vision of myself. But over the last thirty days, You have ministered to my soul. I declare by faith that I am healed, delivered, and transformed. And, I now see myself through Your eyes Lord. Today I declare that according to Psalm 139:13, I am Your masterpiece. I am Your handiwork. I am Your perfected creation. Hallelujah! Father, I pray that You will crown me with honor, favor, and glory. I pray that You will bless me indeed. Father God, I pray, that as I go forth that I will go forth with power and might to do your will, knowing that I am Your perfected craftsmanship. Father God, I pray in the Name of Jesus that You will continue to bless my life. Lord God, I pray that You will continue to bless the words that comes out of my mouth. I pray Lord, that You will continue to use me to glorify Your name. Father, I pray that Your kingdom will come, and Your will be done in my life because I am Your work of art, set on display. Father, I decree and declare that my life will astound and astonish the people who have the honor to get in contact with or come close to me.

Father God, I thank You for my life. I know my worth because I am Your perfected work of art. Father, I totally surrender to Your will for my life. So use me, Lord, to glorify Your Name. Lord, use me as a change agent in the world. Father move through me so that others may be made whole through my story. I thank You for the deliverance that has taken place in my life. I thank You for the healing that has taken place in my life. I thank You for the victory that will be made manifest in my life. For I am Your workmanship, Your masterpiece, Your handiwork, Your perfected craftsmanship, and I thank You for my life. Father God, I seal this prayer in the Name of Jesus. Amen.

You are God's masterpiece. I just want to take a moment to celebrate you for your diligence. The Bible says, "Seest thou a man diligent in his business? He shall stand before kings; he will not stand before mean [average] men" (Proverbs 22:29 (ERV)). Your diligent pursuit for your breakthrough has resulted in great manifestation in your life. I celebrate the transformation that you have encountered. I celebrate the move of God that has taken place in your life. We are going to finish this race.

I seal this series in the Name of Jesus. Father God, I thank You because your work has been completed. Father, I thank You because "Thou Art Beautiful" has been released, and Your daughter now sees herself as a daughter of the King. She now walks in boldness and authority. She walks in victory as a child of the Most High God. Father, I thank You for the transformation that has taken place in the heart, mind, and soul of Your daughter. Lord, I honor You, I glorify You, I worship You, I appreciate You, and I thank You. In Jesus' mighty Name. Amen, amen, and amen.

I want to pause for a moment and encourage you to shoot me an email and send me your testimonial if you have been blessed by this series. If you have received deliverance in any area of your life—if God has moved in your life in any way supernaturally—send me an email. I would love to hear from you. You can reach me at transform@ latoyafonville.com.

Congratulations

Congratulations! Glory to God! You have just completed the Thou Art Beautiful 30-Day Transformation Devotional, and I know that your life has been blessed. I know that God has moved mightily in your life.

I would love to hear your testimonies and feedback. You can email me directly at transform@latoyafonville.com. Also, if you're interested in booking me to speak at your women's events or taking this another step further, we can develop a customized strategy to unleash your destiny through my coaching programs and private coaching sessions. Again, you can visit my website at www.thouartbeautiful.org for more information.

I am so excited for what you have done, and I am so proud of you. Most people would not have taken this step to invest in themselves and be transformed. God put me through a process and a journey to transform my life—and if it wasn't for these declarations, I don't know where I would be. But today, I stand before you as a preacher, transformational speaker, and lifestyle transformational strategist.

It was in my wilderness experience that the Lord Himself began to minister to my spirit and download the confidence of the Kingdom of God into me. It was in my place of brokenness that the Lord began to show Himself mightily and show me myself in His very reflection. I thank the Lord for what He has done in my life, and I pray that my journey towards Kingdom confidence will be the very catalyst that brings about total transformation in your own life.

With that being said, I want to thank you for your support. I pray that this has been a blessing to you. My prayer for you is that you know—with every fiber of your being—that Thou Art Beautiful.

About the Author

LaToya Fonville was born on the beautiful island of St. Martin, but grew up in New York City. She obtained a Bachelor of Science degree in Business Management from the University at Buffalo. During her college years, she overcame her shyness and fear of public speaking and went on to work for a multilevel marketing company, which further helped her to become the excellent communicator that she is today. Having overcome those challenges, LaToya discovered that her passion was teaching, training, and preaching--while inspiring others to discover their purpose in life as well.

Having seen miracles in her own life, LaToya has a grateful heart and loves to worship God. She specializes in working with women who have made every attempt to achieve their goals but are met with constant distractions or roadblocks. Her passion in life is to see women discover their kingdom purpose, overcome obstacles, so that they can be successful in every area of their lives.

LaToya plays many different roles, but her favorite is that of a devoted wife and mother to three brilliant boys. She values family and friends, so it is not surprising that she is a leader in her community. LaToya helps to unearth the entrepreneurial spirit that is in us.

Today, LaToya is a highly sought-after international teacher, preacher, and coach. She is the founder of Essence of Perfection, LLC and LaToya Fonville International, Inc., both with the mission of helping women fulfill their destiny. The challenges that she has overcome in life have inspired her to help other women become victors instead of victims. LaToya writes under the divine inspiration of the Holy Spirit to motivate and propel women forward towards their destiny. Operating on another realm, so that they can have Kingdom Confidence, operate in their God ordained Power, and take Authority in every arena they are called to dominate.

NOTES

Unless otherwise indicated, Scripture quotations are from the Holy Bible, New King James Version:

New King James Bible. (2004). Thomas Nelson (Original work published 1982).

Day 4: I Am Delightful

1. 1. "Delightful Synonyms with Definition: Macmillan Thesaurus." *Synonyms with Definition | Macmillan Thesaurus,* www.macmillanthesaurus.com/us/delightful.

Day 7: I Am Sophisticated

1. "Sophisticated." *Thesaurus.com,* Thesaurus.com, https://www.thesaurus.com/browse/sophisticated.

2. The first part of this prayer was inspired by Sonya Peebles.

Day 8: I Am Perfection

1. "Perfect." *Dictionary.com*, Dictionary.com, https://
    www.dictionary.com/browse/perfect.

Day 11: I Am Capable

1. "Capable." *Dictionary.com*, Dictionary.com, https://
    www.dictionary.com/browse/capable.

Day 14: I Am Incredible

1. "INCREDIBLE: Synonyms of INCREDIBLE by
    Oxford Dictionary on Lexico.com Also Antonyms of
    INCREDIBLE." *Lexico Dictionaries* | English, Lexico
    Dictionaries, www.lexico.com/synonyms/incredible.

Day 15: I Am Remarkable

1. "Remarkable." *Dictionary.com*, Dictionary.com, https://
    www.dictionary.com/browse/remarkable.

Day 18: I Am One of a Kind

1. "One of a kind." *Dictionary.com*, Dictionary.com,
    https://www.dictionary.com/browse/https://www.
    dictionary.com/browse/one--of--a--kind.

Day 19: I Am Virtuous

1. "Virtue." *Dictionary.com,* Dictionary.com, https://www. dictionary.com/browse/virtue.

Day 22: I Am Favored

1. "Favor." *Dictionary.com,* Dictionary.com, https://www. dictionary.com/browse/favor.

Day 24: I Am Complete

1. *Strong's Greek: 4137. Πληρόω (Pléroó) -- to Make Full,* to Complete, biblehub.com/greek/4137.htm.

Day 26: I Am A Conqueror

1. "Reference List - Conqueror." *King James Bible Dictionary,* kingjamesbibledictionary.com/Dictionary/ conqueror.

Day 28: I Am Righteous

1. "Righteous." *Thesaurus.com,* Thesaurus.com, https:// www.thesaurus.com/browse/righteous.

Day 30: I Am A Masterpiece

1. "Masterpiece." *Merriam-Webster,* Merriam-Webster, www.merriam-webster.com/dictionary/masterpiece.

www.ingramcontent.com/pod-product-compliance
Lightning Source LLC
Chambersburg PA
CBHW031253060726
47590CB00003B/890